TABLE OF CONTENTS

TABLE OF CONTENTS

#	SUBJECT	PAGE

#	SUBJECT	PAGE

YEARLY AMOUNT DUE & AMOUNT PAID

YEAR : ....

MONTH	AMOUNT DUE	AMOUNT PAID	UNPAID BALANCE	NOTES
TOTAL				

NOTES

_____

_____

_____

_____

_____

_____

_____

_____

_____

_____

_____

_____

_____

YEARLY AMOUNT DUE & AMOUNT PAID CHART

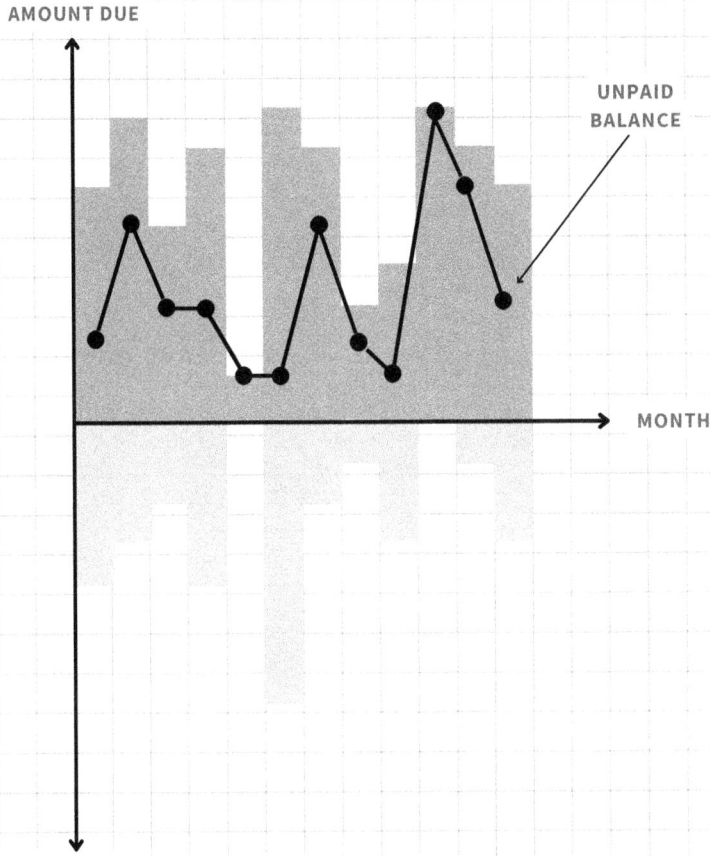

AMOUNT DUE

UNPAID BALANCE

MONTH

AMOUNT PAID

AMOUNT DUE

MONTH

AMOUNT PAID

HOW TO:

BUILD YOUR CHART USING YOUR MONTHLY AMOUNT DUE & AMOUNT PAID SUMMARIES:

- CALCULATE YOUR SCALE USING THE HIGHEST NUMBER IN TERMS OF THE AMOUNT DUE OR THE AMOUNT PAID PER MONTH AND DIVIDE IT BY 10 TO GET THE SIZE OF A SQUARE ON THE Y AXIS
- PLOT YOUR TOTAL MONTHLY AMOUNT DUE AS POSITIVE BARS ON THE Y-AXIS AND YOUR TOTAL MONTHLY AMOUNT PAID AS NEGATIVE BARS ON THE Y-AXIS (DIVIDE THE MONTHLY AMOUNT DUE/AMOUNT PAID BY THE SIZE OF A SQUARE TO FIND THE NUMBER OF SQUARES TO FILL)
- BUILD YOUR UNPAID BALANCE LINE CHART USING YOUR MONTHLY DIFFERENCE

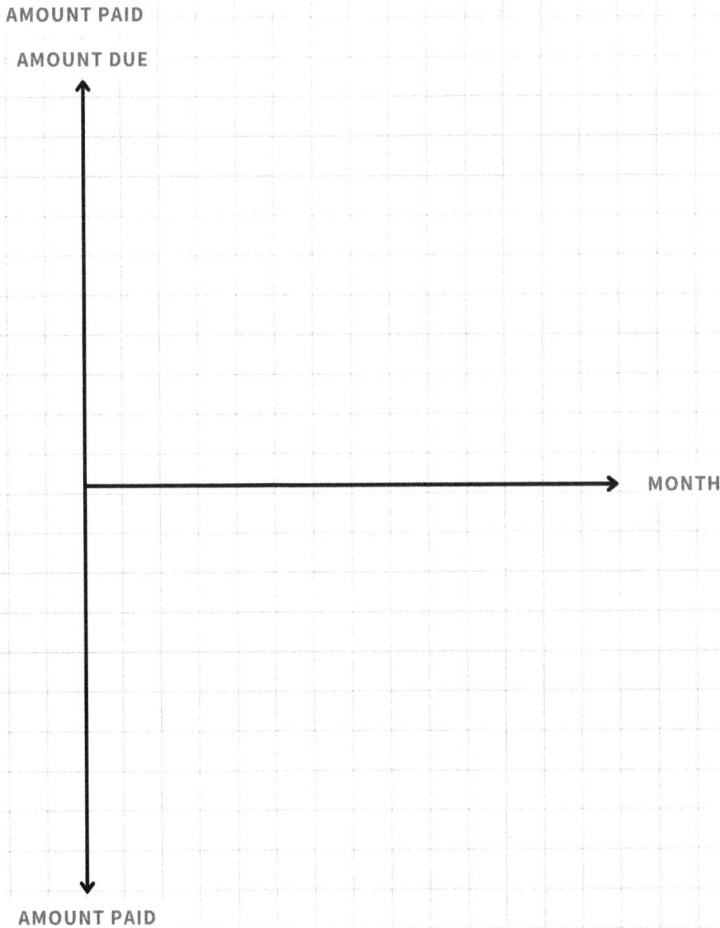

YEAR:

NOTES:

YEARLY AMOUNT DUE & AMOUNT PAID

YEAR : ....

MONTH	AMOUNT DUE	AMOUNT PAID	UNPAID BALANCE	NOTES
TOTAL				

NOTES

_____
_____
_____
_____
_____
_____
_____
_____
_____
_____
_____
_____
_____
_____

YEARLY AMOUNT DUE & AMOUNT PAID CHART

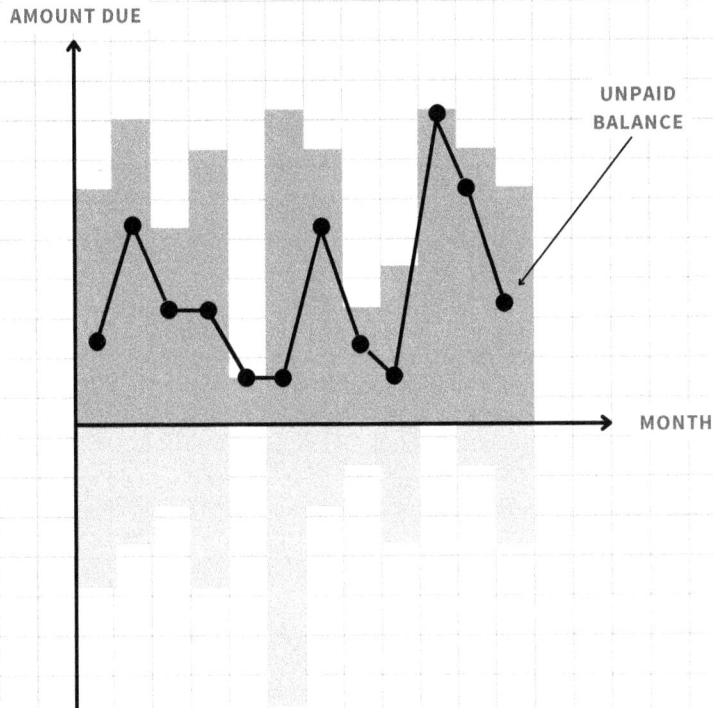

AMOUNT DUE

UNPAID
BALANCE

MONTH

AMOUNT PAID

HOW TO:

BUILD YOUR CHART USING YOUR MONTHLY AMOUNT DUE & AMOUNT PAID SUMMARIES:

- CALCULATE YOUR SCALE USING THE HIGHEST NUMBER IN TERMS OF THE AMOUNT DUE OR THE AMOUNT PAID PER MONTH AND DIVIDE IT BY 10 TO GET THE SIZE OF A SQUARE ON THE Y AXIS
- PLOT YOUR TOTAL MONTHLY AMOUNT DUE AS POSITIVE BARS ON THE Y-AXIS AND YOUR TOTAL MONTHLY AMOUNT PAID AS NEGATIVE BARS ON THE Y-AXIS (DIVIDE THE MONTHLY AMOUNT DUE/AMOUNT PAID BY THE SIZE OF A SQUARE TO FIND THE NUMBER OF SQUARES TO FILL)
- BUILD YOUR UNPAID BALANCE LINE CHART USING YOUR MONTHLY DIFFERENCE

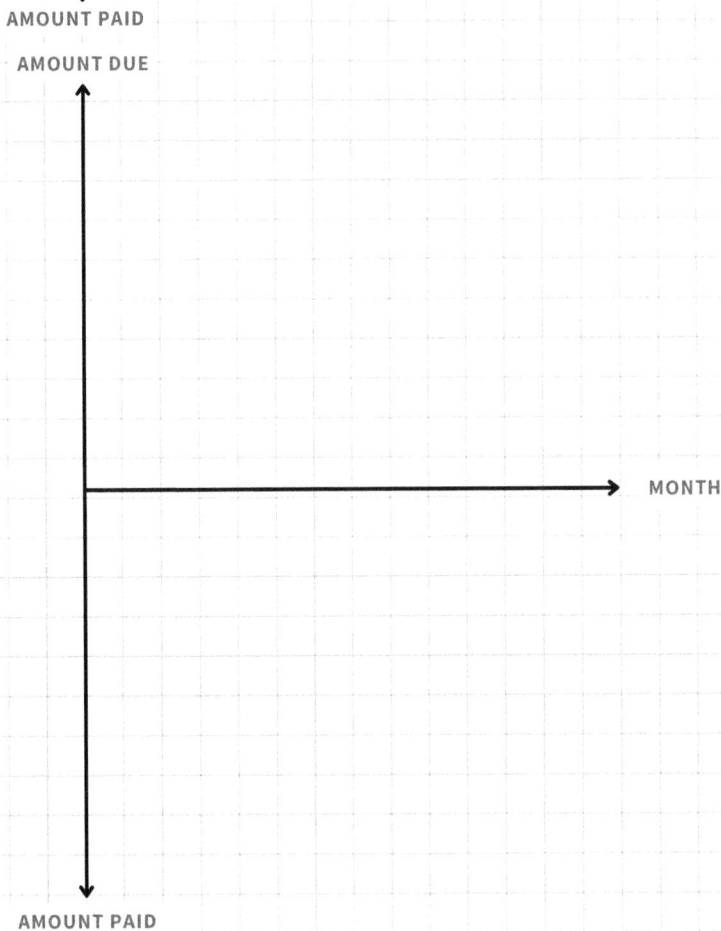

AMOUNT DUE

YEAR:

NOTES:

MONTH

AMOUNT PAID

YEARLY AMOUNT DUE & AMOUNT PAID

YEAR : ....

MONTH	AMOUNT DUE	AMOUNT PAID	UNPAID BALANCE	NOTES
TOTAL				

NOTES

_____
_____
_____
_____
_____
_____
_____
_____
_____
_____
_____
_____
_____
_____
_____

YEARLY AMOUNT DUE & AMOUNT PAID CHART

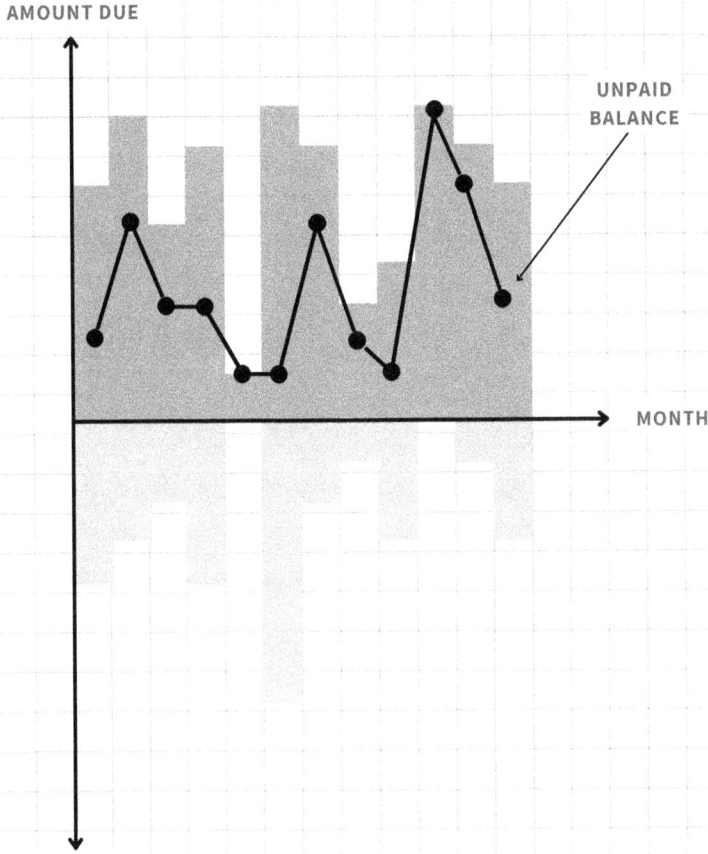

AMOUNT DUE

UNPAID
BALANCE

MONTH

AMOUNT PAID

HOW TO:
BUILD YOUR CHART USING YOUR MONTHLY
AMOUNT DUE & AMOUNT PAID SUMMARIES:

- CALCULATE YOUR SCALE USING THE
  HIGHEST NUMBER IN TERMS OF THE
  AMOUNT DUE OR THE AMOUNT PAID PER
  MONTH AND DIVIDE IT BY 10 TO GET THE
  SIZE OF A SQUARE ON THE Y AXIS
- PLOT YOUR TOTAL MONTHLY AMOUNT DUE
  AS POSITIVE BARS ON THE Y-AXIS AND YOUR
  TOTAL MONTHLY AMOUNT PAID AS NEGATIVE
  BARS ON THE Y-AXIS (DIVIDE THE MONTHLY
  AMOUNT DUE/AMOUNT PAID BY THE SIZE OF
  A SQUARE TO FIND THE NUMBER OF
  SQUARES TO FILL)
- BUILD YOUR UNPAID BALANCE LINE CHART
  USING YOUR MONTHLY DIFFERENCE

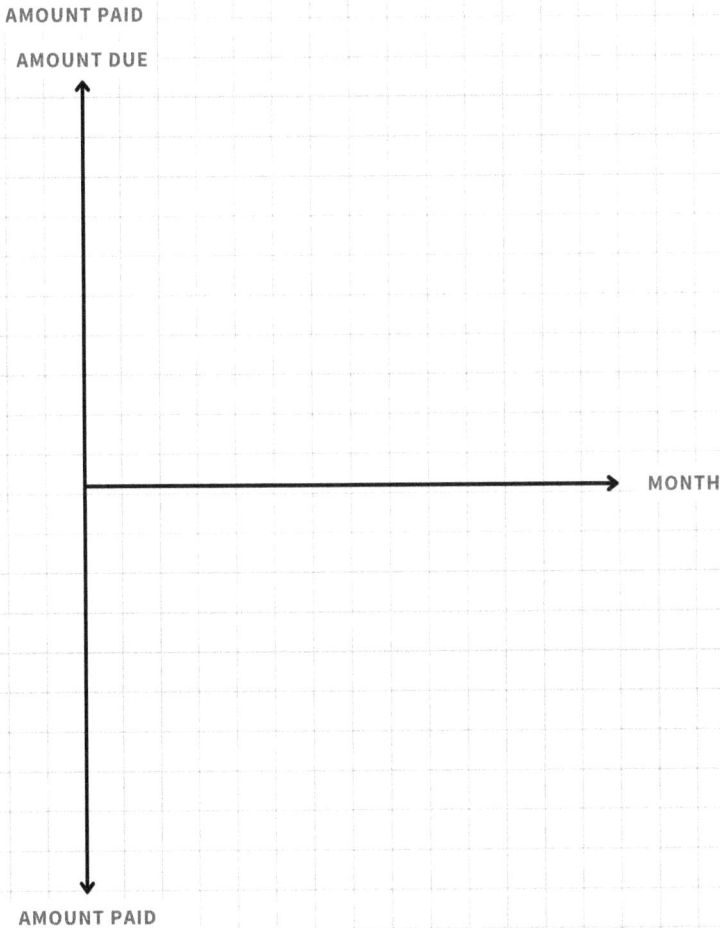

AMOUNT DUE

MONTH

AMOUNT PAID

YEAR:

NOTES:

YEARLY AMOUNT DUE & AMOUNT PAID

YEAR : ....

MONTH	AMOUNT DUE	AMOUNT PAID	UNPAID BALANCE	NOTES
TOTAL				

NOTES

_____

_____

_____

_____

_____

_____

_____

_____

_____

_____

_____

_____

_____

_____

YEARLY AMOUNT DUE & AMOUNT PAID CHART

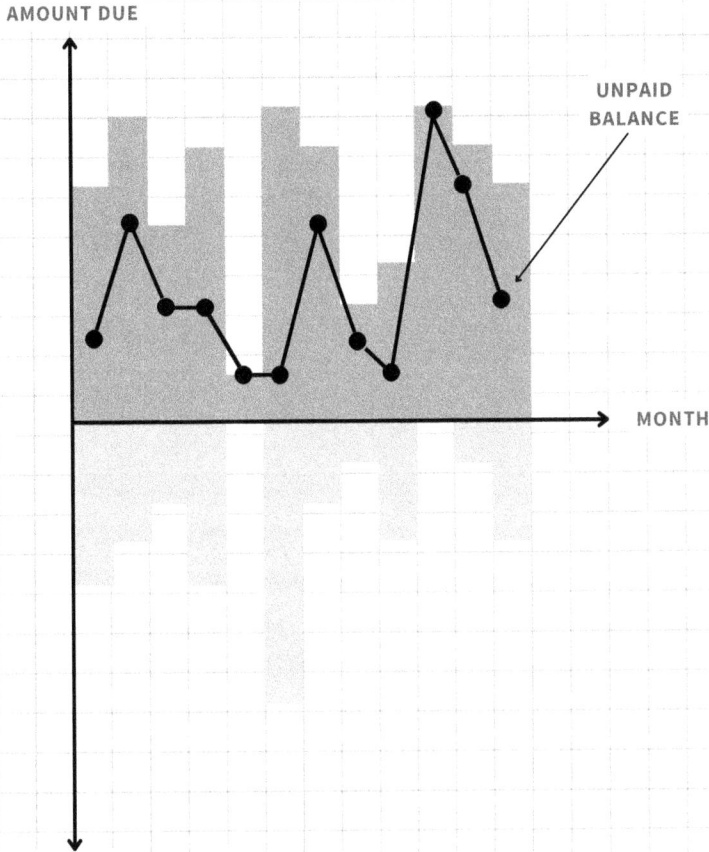

AMOUNT DUE

UNPAID
BALANCE

MONTH

AMOUNT PAID

HOW TO:

BUILD YOUR CHART USING YOUR MONTHLY
AMOUNT DUE & AMOUNT PAID SUMMARIES:

- CALCULATE YOUR SCALE USING THE
  HIGHEST NUMBER IN TERMS OF THE
  AMOUNT DUE OR THE AMOUNT PAID PER
  MONTH AND DIVIDE IT BY 10 TO GET THE
  SIZE OF A SQUARE ON THE Y AXIS
- PLOT YOUR TOTAL MONTHLY AMOUNT DUE
  AS POSITIVE BARS ON THE Y-AXIS AND YOUR
  TOTAL MONTHLY AMOUNT PAID AS NEGATIVE
  BARS ON THE Y-AXIS (DIVIDE THE MONTHLY
  AMOUNT DUE/AMOUNT PAID BY THE SIZE OF
  A SQUARE TO FIND THE NUMBER OF
  SQUARES TO FILL)
- BUILD YOUR UNPAID BALANCE LINE CHART
  USING YOUR MONTHLY DIFFERENCE

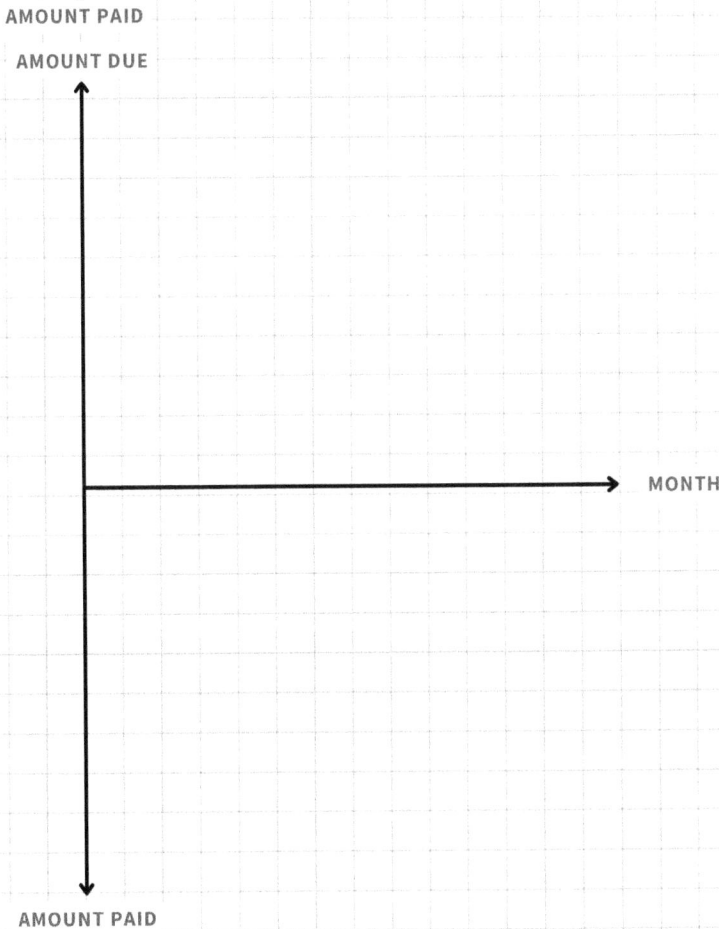

AMOUNT DUE

YEAR:

NOTES:

MONTH

AMOUNT PAID

YEARLY AMOUNT DUE & AMOUNT PAID

YEAR : ....

MONTH	AMOUNT DUE	AMOUNT PAID	UNPAID BALANCE	NOTES
TOTAL				

NOTES

_____
_____
_____
_____
_____
_____
_____
_____
_____
_____
_____
_____
_____

YEARLY AMOUNT DUE & AMOUNT PAID CHART

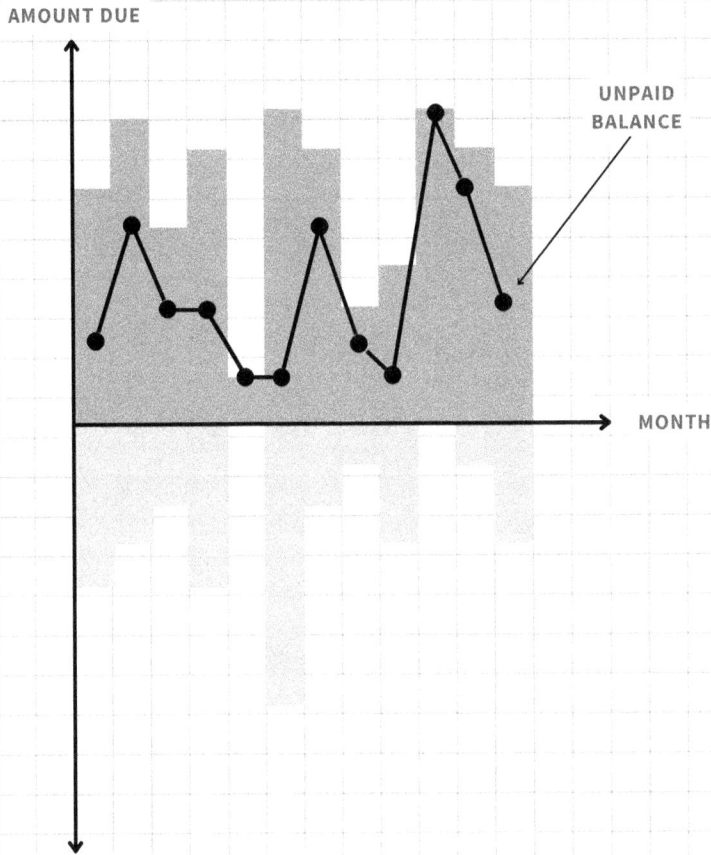

AMOUNT DUE

UNPAID
BALANCE

MONTH

AMOUNT PAID

HOW TO:
BUILD YOUR CHART USING YOUR MONTHLY AMOUNT DUE & AMOUNT PAID SUMMARIES:

- CALCULATE YOUR SCALE USING THE HIGHEST NUMBER IN TERMS OF THE AMOUNT DUE OR THE AMOUNT PAID PER MONTH AND DIVIDE IT BY 10 TO GET THE SIZE OF A SQUARE ON THE Y AXIS
- PLOT YOUR TOTAL MONTHLY AMOUNT DUE AS POSITIVE BARS ON THE Y-AXIS AND YOUR TOTAL MONTHLY AMOUNT PAID AS NEGATIVE BARS ON THE Y-AXIS (DIVIDE THE MONTHLY AMOUNT DUE/AMOUNT PAID BY THE SIZE OF A SQUARE TO FIND THE NUMBER OF SQUARES TO FILL)
- BUILD YOUR UNPAID BALANCE LINE CHART USING YOUR MONTHLY DIFFERENCE

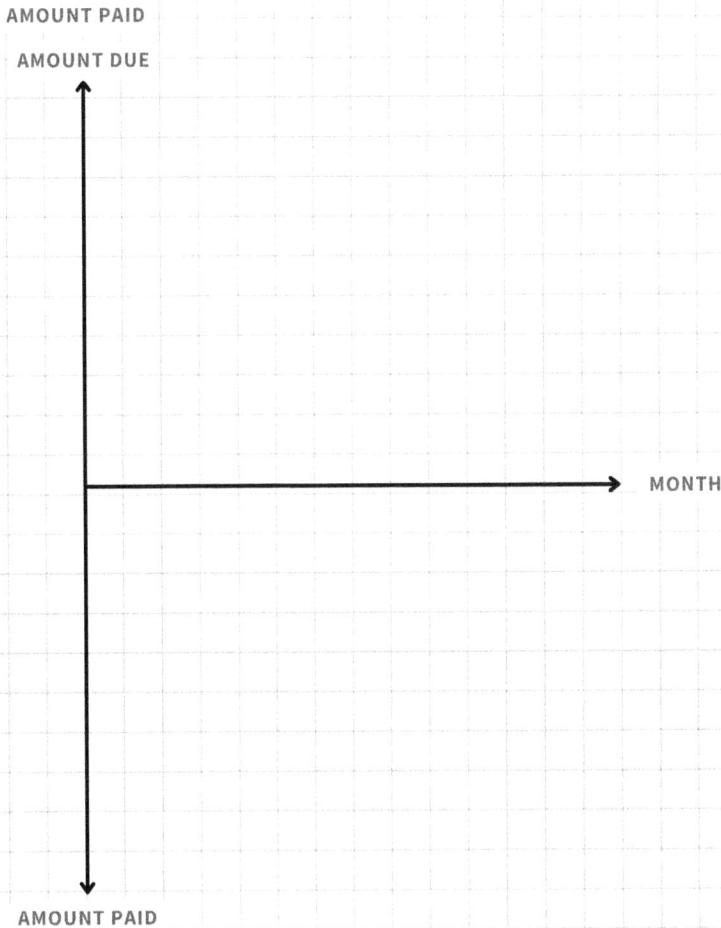

AMOUNT DUE

YEAR:

NOTES:

MONTH

AMOUNT PAID

YEARLY AMOUNT DUE & AMOUNT PAID

YEAR : ....

MONTH	AMOUNT DUE	AMOUNT PAID	UNPAID BALANCE	NOTES
TOTAL				

NOTES

_____
_____
_____
_____
_____
_____
_____
_____
_____
_____
_____
_____
_____
_____

YEARLY AMOUNT DUE & AMOUNT PAID CHART

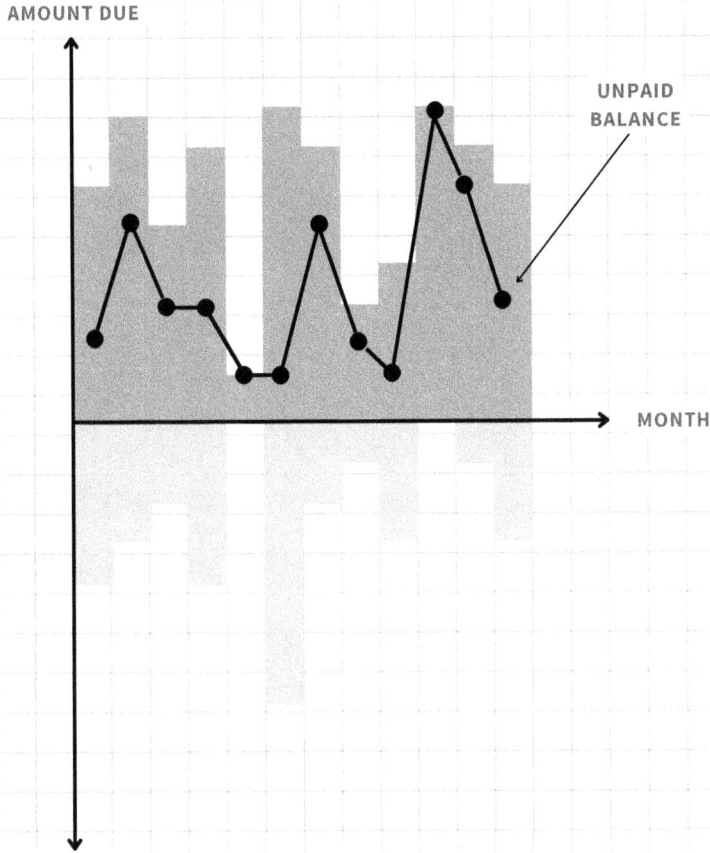

AMOUNT DUE

UNPAID
BALANCE

MONTH

HOW TO:

BUILD YOUR CHART USING YOUR MONTHLY
AMOUNT DUE & AMOUNT PAID SUMMARIES:

- CALCULATE YOUR SCALE USING THE
  HIGHEST NUMBER IN TERMS OF THE
  AMOUNT DUE OR THE AMOUNT PAID PER
  MONTH AND DIVIDE IT BY 10 TO GET THE
  SIZE OF A SQUARE ON THE Y AXIS
- PLOT YOUR TOTAL MONTHLY AMOUNT DUE
  AS POSITIVE BARS ON THE Y-AXIS AND YOUR
  TOTAL MONTHLY AMOUNT PAID AS NEGATIVE
  BARS ON THE Y-AXIS (DIVIDE THE MONTHLY
  AMOUNT DUE/AMOUNT PAID BY THE SIZE OF
  A SQUARE TO FIND THE NUMBER OF
  SQUARES TO FILL)
- BUILD YOUR UNPAID BALANCE LINE CHART
  USING YOUR MONTHLY DIFFERENCE

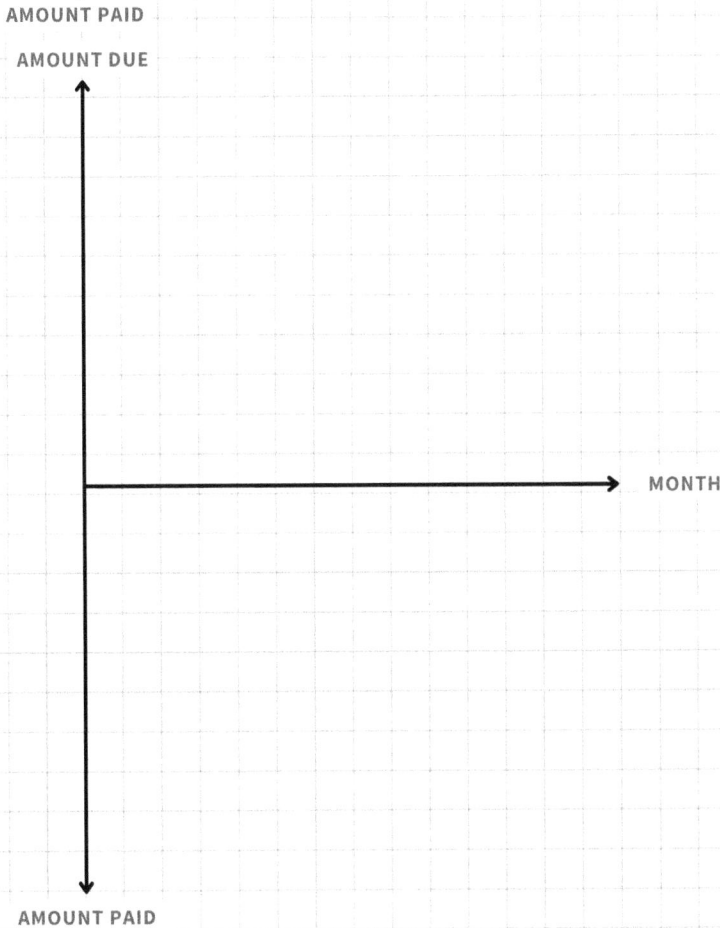

AMOUNT PAID

AMOUNT DUE

YEAR:

NOTES:

MONTH

AMOUNT PAID

12

YEARLY AMOUNT DUE & AMOUNT PAID

YEAR : ....

MONTH	AMOUNT DUE	AMOUNT PAID	UNPAID BALANCE	NOTES
TOTAL				

NOTES

_____
_____
_____
_____
_____
_____
_____
_____
_____
_____
_____
_____
_____

YEARLY AMOUNT DUE & AMOUNT PAID CHART

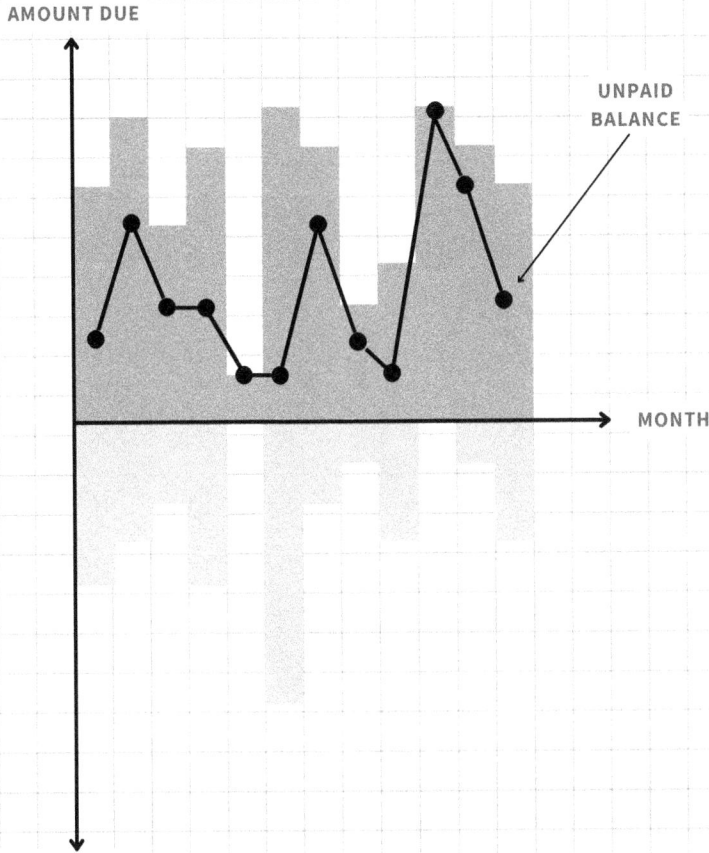

AMOUNT DUE

UNPAID
BALANCE

MONTH

AMOUNT PAID

AMOUNT DUE

MONTH

AMOUNT PAID

HOW TO:

BUILD YOUR CHART USING YOUR MONTHLY
AMOUNT DUE & AMOUNT PAID SUMMARIES:

- CALCULATE YOUR SCALE USING THE
  HIGHEST NUMBER IN TERMS OF THE
  AMOUNT DUE OR THE AMOUNT PAID PER
  MONTH AND DIVIDE IT BY 10 TO GET THE
  SIZE OF A SQUARE ON THE Y AXIS
- PLOT YOUR TOTAL MONTHLY AMOUNT DUE
  AS POSITIVE BARS ON THE Y-AXIS AND YOUR
  TOTAL MONTHLY AMOUNT PAID AS NEGATIVE
  BARS ON THE Y-AXIS (DIVIDE THE MONTHLY
  AMOUNT DUE/AMOUNT PAID BY THE SIZE OF
  A SQUARE TO FIND THE NUMBER OF
  SQUARES TO FILL)
- BUILD YOUR UNPAID BALANCE LINE CHART
  USING YOUR MONTHLY DIFFERENCE

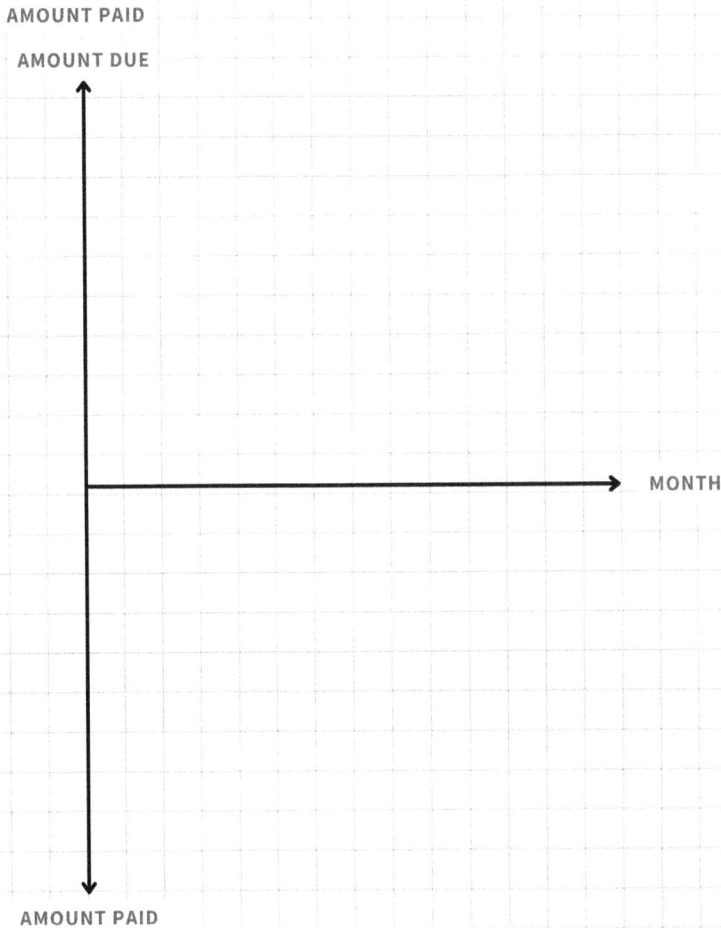

YEAR:

NOTES:

14

YEARLY AMOUNT DUE & AMOUNT PAID

YEAR : ....

MONTH	AMOUNT DUE	AMOUNT PAID	UNPAID BALANCE	NOTES
TOTAL				

NOTES

_____
_____
_____
_____
_____
_____
_____
_____
_____
_____
_____
_____
_____

YEARLY AMOUNT DUE & AMOUNT PAID CHART

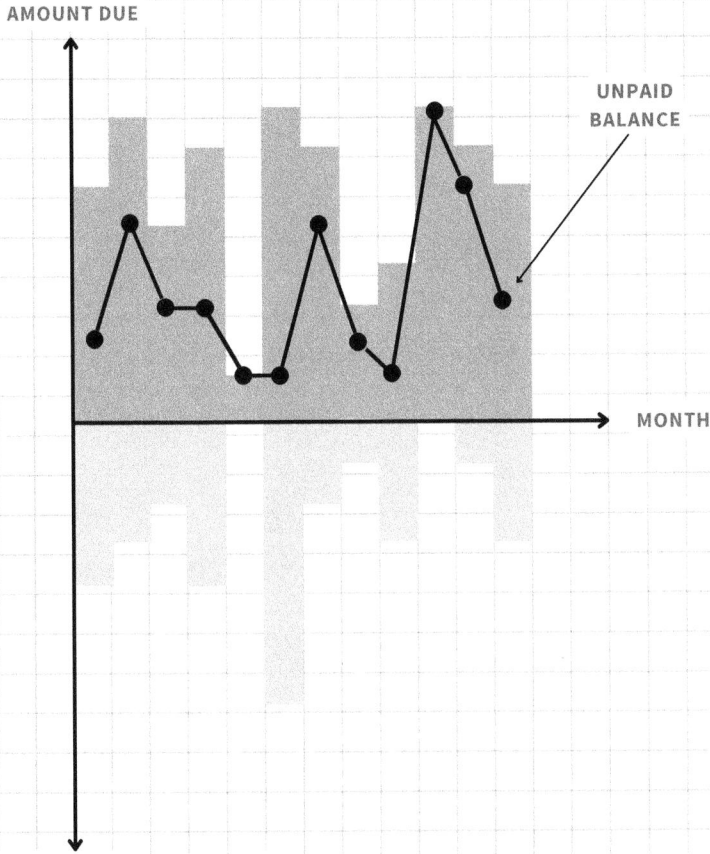

AMOUNT DUE

UNPAID BALANCE

MONTH

AMOUNT PAID

HOW TO:

BUILD YOUR CHART USING YOUR MONTHLY AMOUNT DUE & AMOUNT PAID SUMMARIES:

- CALCULATE YOUR SCALE USING THE HIGHEST NUMBER IN TERMS OF THE AMOUNT DUE OR THE AMOUNT PAID PER MONTH AND DIVIDE IT BY 10 TO GET THE SIZE OF A SQUARE ON THE Y AXIS
- PLOT YOUR TOTAL MONTHLY AMOUNT DUE AS POSITIVE BARS ON THE Y-AXIS AND YOUR TOTAL MONTHLY AMOUNT PAID AS NEGATIVE BARS ON THE Y-AXIS (DIVIDE THE MONTHLY AMOUNT DUE/AMOUNT PAID BY THE SIZE OF A SQUARE TO FIND THE NUMBER OF SQUARES TO FILL)
- BUILD YOUR UNPAID BALANCE LINE CHART USING YOUR MONTHLY DIFFERENCE

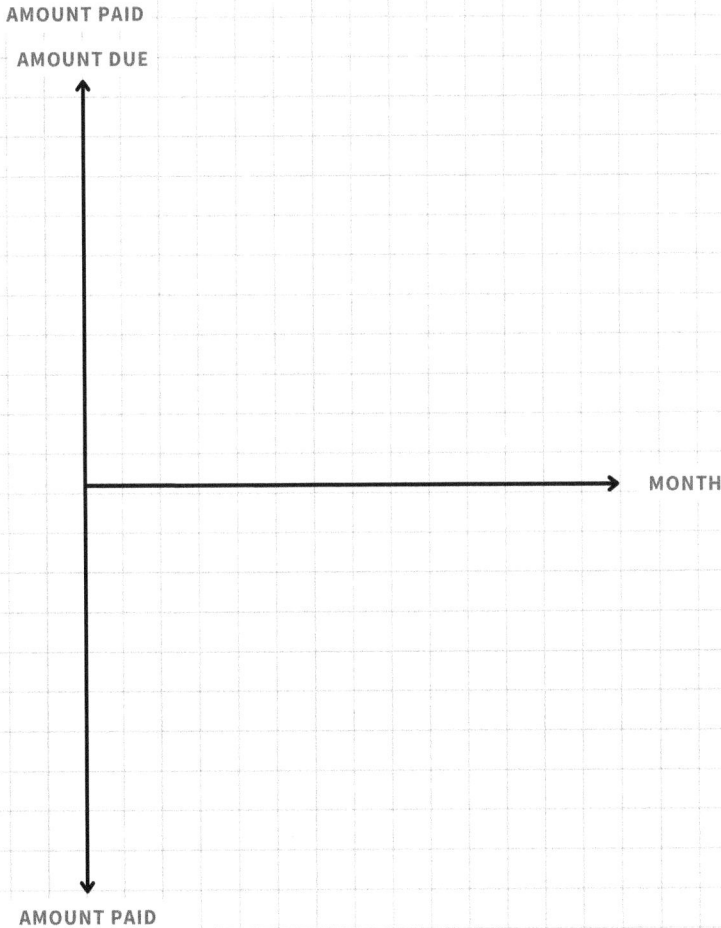

AMOUNT DUE

YEAR:

NOTES:

MONTH

AMOUNT PAID

MONTHLY BILL PAYMENT

MONTH:						YEAR:

PAID	BILL DESCRIPTION	DUE DATE	AMOUNT DUE	AMOUNT PAID	UNPAID BALANCE	NOTES
☐						
☐						
☐						
☐						
☐						
☐						
☐						
☐						
☐						
☐						
☐						
☐						
☐						
☐						
☐						
☐						
☐						
☐						
☐						
☐						
☐						
☐						
☐						
	TOTAL					

MONTHLY BILL PAYMENT

MONTH: **YEAR:**

PAID	BILL DESCRIPTION	DUE DATE	AMOUNT DUE	AMOUNT PAID	UNPAID BALANCE	NOTES
☐						
☐						
☐						
☐						
☐						
☐						
☐						
☐						
☐						
☐						
☐						
☐						
☐						
☐						
☐						
☐						
☐						
☐						
☐						
☐						
☐						
☐						
TOTAL						

MONTHLY BILL PAYMENT

MONTH:						YEAR:

PAID	BILL DESCRIPTION	DUE DATE	AMOUNT DUE	AMOUNT PAID	UNPAID BALANCE	NOTES
☐						
☐						
☐						
☐						
☐						
☐						
☐						
☐						
☐						
☐						
☐						
☐						
☐						
☐						
☐						
☐						
☐						
☐						
☐						
☐						
☐						
☐						
☐						
	TOTAL					

MONTHLY BILL PAYMENT

MONTH:					YEAR:	

PAID	BILL DESCRIPTION	DUE DATE	AMOUNT DUE	AMOUNT PAID	UNPAID BALANCE	NOTES
☐						
☐						
☐						
☐						
☐						
☐						
☐						
☐						
☐						
☐						
☐						
☐						
☐						
☐						
☐						
☐						
☐						
☐						
☐						
☐						
☐						
☐						
☐						
TOTAL						

MONTHLY BILL PAYMENT

MONTH:						YEAR:

PAID	BILL DESCRIPTION	DUE DATE	AMOUNT DUE	AMOUNT PAID	UNPAID BALANCE	NOTES
☐						
☐						
☐						
☐						
☐						
☐						
☐						
☐						
☐						
☐						
☐						
☐						
☐						
☐						
☐						
☐						
☐						
☐						
☐						
☐						
☐						
☐						
☐						
	TOTAL					

MONTHLY BILL PAYMENT

MONTH:					YEAR:	

PAID	BILL DESCRIPTION	DUE DATE	AMOUNT DUE	AMOUNT PAID	UNPAID BALANCE	NOTES
☐						
☐						
☐						
☐						
☐						
☐						
☐						
☐						
☐						
☐						
☐						
☐						
☐						
☐						
☐						
☐						
☐						
☐						
☐						
☐						
☐						
☐						
☐						
☐						
☐						
	TOTAL					

MONTHLY BILL PAYMENT

MONTH:						YEAR:

PAID	BILL DESCRIPTION	DUE DATE	AMOUNT DUE	AMOUNT PAID	UNPAID BALANCE	NOTES
☐						
☐						
☐						
☐						
☐						
☐						
☐						
☐						
☐						
☐						
☐						
☐						
☐						
☐						
☐						
☐						
☐						
☐						
☐						
☐						
☐						
☐						
☐						
	TOTAL					

MONTHLY BILL PAYMENT

MONTH:					YEAR:	

PAID	BILL DESCRIPTION	DUE DATE	AMOUNT DUE	AMOUNT PAID	UNPAID BALANCE	NOTES
☐						
☐						
☐						
☐						
☐						
☐						
☐						
☐						
☐						
☐						
☐						
☐						
☐						
☐						
☐						
☐						
☐						
☐						
☐						
☐						
☐						
☐						
☐						
	TOTAL					

MONTHLY BILL PAYMENT

MONTH:					YEAR:	

PAID	BILL DESCRIPTION	DUE DATE	AMOUNT DUE	AMOUNT PAID	UNPAID BALANCE	NOTES
☐						
☐						
☐						
☐						
☐						
☐						
☐						
☐						
☐						
☐						
☐						
☐						
☐						
☐						
☐						
☐						
☐						
☐						
☐						
☐						
☐						
☐						
☐						
	TOTAL					

MONTHLY BILL PAYMENT

MONTH:					YEAR:

PAID	BILL DESCRIPTION	DUE DATE	AMOUNT DUE	AMOUNT PAID	UNPAID BALANCE	NOTES
☐						
☐						
☐						
☐						
☐						
☐						
☐						
☐						
☐						
☐						
☐						
☐						
☐						
☐						
☐						
☐						
☐						
☐						
☐						
☐						
☐						
☐						
☐						
	TOTAL					

MONTHLY BILL PAYMENT

| MONTH: | | | | | | YEAR: |

PAID	BILL DESCRIPTION	DUE DATE	AMOUNT DUE	AMOUNT PAID	UNPAID BALANCE	NOTES
☐						
☐						
☐						
☐						
☐						
☐						
☐						
☐						
☐						
☐						
☐						
☐						
☐						
☐						
☐						
☐						
☐						
☐						
☐						
☐						
☐						
☐						
☐						
☐						
	TOTAL					

MONTHLY BILL PAYMENT

MONTH:					YEAR:	

PAID	BILL DESCRIPTION	DUE DATE	AMOUNT DUE	AMOUNT PAID	UNPAID BALANCE	NOTES
☐						
☐						
☐						
☐						
☐						
☐						
☐						
☐						
☐						
☐						
☐						
☐						
☐						
☐						
☐						
☐						
☐						
☐						
☐						
☐						
☐						
☐						
☐						
☐						
	TOTAL					

_____

_____

_____

_____

MONTHLY BILL PAYMENT

MONTH: **YEAR:**

PAID	BILL DESCRIPTION	DUE DATE	AMOUNT DUE	AMOUNT PAID	UNPAID BALANCE	NOTES
☐						
☐						
☐						
☐						
☐						
☐						
☐						
☐						
☐						
☐						
☐						
☐						
☐						
☐						
☐						
☐						
☐						
☐						
☐						
☐						
☐						
☐						
☐						
☐						
	TOTAL					

MONTHLY BILL PAYMENT

MONTH:					YEAR:	

PAID	BILL DESCRIPTION	DUE DATE	AMOUNT DUE	AMOUNT PAID	UNPAID BALANCE	NOTES
☐						
☐						
☐						
☐						
☐						
☐						
☐						
☐						
☐						
☐						
☐						
☐						
☐						
☐						
☐						
☐						
☐						
☐						
☐						
☐						
☐						
☐						
	TOTAL					

_____
_____
_____
_____

MONTHLY BILL PAYMENT

MONTH:					YEAR:	

PAID	BILL DESCRIPTION	DUE DATE	AMOUNT DUE	AMOUNT PAID	UNPAID BALANCE	NOTES
☐						
☐						
☐						
☐						
☐						
☐						
☐						
☐						
☐						
☐						
☐						
☐						
☐						
☐						
☐						
☐						
☐						
☐						
☐						
☐						
☐						
☐						
☐						
	TOTAL					

MONTHLY BILL PAYMENT

MONTH:						YEAR:

PAID	BILL DESCRIPTION	DUE DATE	AMOUNT DUE	AMOUNT PAID	UNPAID BALANCE	NOTES
☐						
☐						
☐						
☐						
☐						
☐						
☐						
☐						
☐						
☐						
☐						
☐						
☐						
☐						
☐						
☐						
☐						
☐						
☐						
☐						
☐						
☐						
☐						
	TOTAL					

MONTHLY BILL PAYMENT

MONTH: **YEAR:**

PAID	BILL DESCRIPTION	DUE DATE	AMOUNT DUE	AMOUNT PAID	UNPAID BALANCE	NOTES
☐						
☐						
☐						
☐						
☐						
☐						
☐						
☐						
☐						
☐						
☐						
☐						
☐						
☐						
☐						
☐						
☐						
☐						
☐						
☐						
☐						
☐						
☐						
	TOTAL					

MONTHLY BILL PAYMENT

MONTH:					YEAR:	

PAID	BILL DESCRIPTION	DUE DATE	AMOUNT DUE	AMOUNT PAID	UNPAID BALANCE	NOTES
☐						
☐						
☐						
☐						
☐						
☐						
☐						
☐						
☐						
☐						
☐						
☐						
☐						
☐						
☐						
☐						
☐						
☐						
☐						
☐						
☐						
☐						
☐						
	TOTAL					

MONTHLY BILL PAYMENT

MONTH:						YEAR:

PAID	BILL DESCRIPTION	DUE DATE	AMOUNT DUE	AMOUNT PAID	UNPAID BALANCE	NOTES
☐						
☐						
☐						
☐						
☐						
☐						
☐						
☐						
☐						
☐						
☐						
☐						
☐						
☐						
☐						
☐						
☐						
☐						
☐						
☐						
☐						
☐						
☐						
	TOTAL					

MONTHLY BILL PAYMENT

MONTH:					YEAR:	

PAID	BILL DESCRIPTION	DUE DATE	AMOUNT DUE	AMOUNT PAID	UNPAID BALANCE	NOTES
☐						
☐						
☐						
☐						
☐						
☐						
☐						
☐						
☐						
☐						
☐						
☐						
☐						
☐						
☐						
☐						
☐						
☐						
☐						
☐						
☐						
☐						
☐						
	TOTAL					

MONTHLY BILL PAYMENT

MONTH:						YEAR:

PAID	BILL DESCRIPTION	DUE DATE	AMOUNT DUE	AMOUNT PAID	UNPAID BALANCE	NOTES
☐						
☐						
☐						
☐						
☐						
☐						
☐						
☐						
☐						
☐						
☐						
☐						
☐						
☐						
☐						
☐						
☐						
☐						
☐						
☐						
☐						
☐						
☐						
	TOTAL					

MONTHLY BILL PAYMENT

MONTH:						YEAR:

PAID	BILL DESCRIPTION	DUE DATE	AMOUNT DUE	AMOUNT PAID	UNPAID BALANCE	NOTES
☐						
☐						
☐						
☐						
☐						
☐						
☐						
☐						
☐						
☐						
☐						
☐						
☐						
☐						
☐						
☐						
☐						
☐						
☐						
☐						
☐						
☐						
☐						
	TOTAL					

MONTHLY BILL PAYMENT

MONTH:						YEAR:

PAID	BILL DESCRIPTION	DUE DATE	AMOUNT DUE	AMOUNT PAID	UNPAID BALANCE	NOTES
☐						
☐						
☐						
☐						
☐						
☐						
☐						
☐						
☐						
☐						
☐						
☐						
☐						
☐						
☐						
☐						
☐						
☐						
☐						
☐						
☐						
☐						
	TOTAL					

MONTHLY BILL PAYMENT

| MONTH: | | | | | YEAR: | |

PAID	BILL DESCRIPTION	DUE DATE	AMOUNT DUE	AMOUNT PAID	UNPAID BALANCE	NOTES
☐						
☐						
☐						
☐						
☐						
☐						
☐						
☐						
☐						
☐						
☐						
☐						
☐						
☐						
☐						
☐						
☐						
☐						
☐						
☐						
☐						
☐						
	TOTAL					

MONTHLY BILL PAYMENT

MONTH:						YEAR:

PAID	BILL DESCRIPTION	DUE DATE	AMOUNT DUE	AMOUNT PAID	UNPAID BALANCE	NOTES
☐						
☐						
☐						
☐						
☐						
☐						
☐						
☐						
☐						
☐						
☐						
☐						
☐						
☐						
☐						
☐						
☐						
☐						
☐						
☐						
☐						
☐						
☐						
	TOTAL					

MONTHLY BILL PAYMENT

MONTH:					YEAR:	

PAID	BILL DESCRIPTION	DUE DATE	AMOUNT DUE	AMOUNT PAID	UNPAID BALANCE	NOTES
☐						
☐						
☐						
☐						
☐						
☐						
☐						
☐						
☐						
☐						
☐						
☐						
☐						
☐						
☐						
☐						
☐						
☐						
☐						
☐						
☐						
☐						
	TOTAL					

MONTHLY BILL PAYMENT

MONTH:					YEAR:	

PAID	BILL DESCRIPTION	DUE DATE	AMOUNT DUE	AMOUNT PAID	UNPAID BALANCE	NOTES
☐						
☐						
☐						
☐						
☐						
☐						
☐						
☐						
☐						
☐						
☐						
☐						
☐						
☐						
☐						
☐						
☐						
☐						
☐						
☐						
☐						
☐						
☐						
	TOTAL					

MONTHLY BILL PAYMENT

MONTH:					YEAR:	

PAID	BILL DESCRIPTION	DUE DATE	AMOUNT DUE	AMOUNT PAID	UNPAID BALANCE	NOTES
☐						
☐						
☐						
☐						
☐						
☐						
☐						
☐						
☐						
☐						
☐						
☐						
☐						
☐						
☐						
☐						
☐						
☐						
☐						
☐						
☐						
☐						
☐						
	TOTAL					

MONTHLY BILL PAYMENT

MONTH:					YEAR:	

PAID	BILL DESCRIPTION	DUE DATE	AMOUNT DUE	AMOUNT PAID	UNPAID BALANCE	NOTES
☐						
☐						
☐						
☐						
☐						
☐						
☐						
☐						
☐						
☐						
☐						
☐						
☐						
☐						
☐						
☐						
☐						
☐						
☐						
☐						
☐						
☐						
	TOTAL					

_____

_____

_____

_____

MONTHLY BILL PAYMENT

MONTH:					YEAR:	

PAID	BILL DESCRIPTION	DUE DATE	AMOUNT DUE	AMOUNT PAID	UNPAID BALANCE	NOTES
☐						
☐						
☐						
☐						
☐						
☐						
☐						
☐						
☐						
☐						
☐						
☐						
☐						
☐						
☐						
☐						
☐						
☐						
☐						
☐						
☐						
☐						
☐						
	TOTAL					

MONTHLY BILL PAYMENT

MONTH:					YEAR:	

PAID	BILL DESCRIPTION	DUE DATE	AMOUNT DUE	AMOUNT PAID	UNPAID BALANCE	NOTES
☐						
☐						
☐						
☐						
☐						
☐						
☐						
☐						
☐						
☐						
☐						
☐						
☐						
☐						
☐						
☐						
☐						
☐						
☐						
☐						
☐						
☐						
☐						
	TOTAL					

MONTHLY BILL PAYMENT

MONTH:						YEAR:

PAID	BILL DESCRIPTION	DUE DATE	AMOUNT DUE	AMOUNT PAID	UNPAID BALANCE	NOTES
☐						
☐						
☐						
☐						
☐						
☐						
☐						
☐						
☐						
☐						
☐						
☐						
☐						
☐						
☐						
☐						
☐						
☐						
☐						
☐						
☐						
☐						
☐						
☐						
	TOTAL					

MONTHLY BILL PAYMENT

MONTH:						YEAR:

PAID	BILL DESCRIPTION	DUE DATE	AMOUNT DUE	AMOUNT PAID	UNPAID BALANCE	NOTES
☐						
☐						
☐						
☐						
☐						
☐						
☐						
☐						
☐						
☐						
☐						
☐						
☐						
☐						
☐						
☐						
☐						
☐						
☐						
☐						
☐						
☐						
☐						
☐						
	TOTAL					

MONTHLY BILL PAYMENT

MONTH:					YEAR:	

PAID	BILL DESCRIPTION	DUE DATE	AMOUNT DUE	AMOUNT PAID	UNPAID BALANCE	NOTES
☐						
☐						
☐						
☐						
☐						
☐						
☐						
☐						
☐						
☐						
☐						
☐						
☐						
☐						
☐						
☐						
☐						
☐						
☐						
☐						
☐						
☐						
☐						
	TOTAL					

MONTHLY BILL PAYMENT

MONTH:						YEAR:

PAID	BILL DESCRIPTION	DUE DATE	AMOUNT DUE	AMOUNT PAID	UNPAID BALANCE	NOTES
☐						
☐						
☐						
☐						
☐						
☐						
☐						
☐						
☐						
☐						
☐						
☐						
☐						
☐						
☐						
☐						
☐						
☐						
☐						
☐						
☐						
☐						
☐						
	TOTAL					

MONTHLY BILL PAYMENT

MONTH:					YEAR:	

PAID	BILL DESCRIPTION	DUE DATE	AMOUNT DUE	AMOUNT PAID	UNPAID BALANCE	NOTES
☐						
☐						
☐						
☐						
☐						
☐						
☐						
☐						
☐						
☐						
☐						
☐						
☐						
☐						
☐						
☐						
☐						
☐						
☐						
☐						
☐						
☐						
☐						
	TOTAL					

MONTHLY BILL PAYMENT

MONTH:						YEAR:

PAID	BILL DESCRIPTION	DUE DATE	AMOUNT DUE	AMOUNT PAID	UNPAID BALANCE	NOTES
☐						
☐						
☐						
☐						
☐						
☐						
☐						
☐						
☐						
☐						
☐						
☐						
☐						
☐						
☐						
☐						
☐						
☐						
☐						
☐						
☐						
☐						
	TOTAL					

MONTHLY BILL PAYMENT

| MONTH: | | | | | YEAR: | |

PAID	BILL DESCRIPTION	DUE DATE	AMOUNT DUE	AMOUNT PAID	UNPAID BALANCE	NOTES
☐						
☐						
☐						
☐						
☐						
☐						
☐						
☐						
☐						
☐						
☐						
☐						
☐						
☐						
☐						
☐						
☐						
☐						
☐						
☐						
☐						
☐						
☐						
	TOTAL					

MONTHLY BILL PAYMENT

MONTH:						YEAR:

PAID	BILL DESCRIPTION	DUE DATE	AMOUNT DUE	AMOUNT PAID	UNPAID BALANCE	NOTES
☐						
☐						
☐						
☐						
☐						
☐						
☐						
☐						
☐						
☐						
☐						
☐						
☐						
☐						
☐						
☐						
☐						
☐						
☐						
☐						
☐						
☐						
☐						
	TOTAL					

MONTHLY BILL PAYMENT

MONTH:					YEAR:	

PAID	BILL DESCRIPTION	DUE DATE	AMOUNT DUE	AMOUNT PAID	UNPAID BALANCE	NOTES
☐						
☐						
☐						
☐						
☐						
☐						
☐						
☐						
☐						
☐						
☐						
☐						
☐						
☐						
☐						
☐						
☐						
☐						
☐						
☐						
☐						
☐						
☐						
	TOTAL					

MONTHLY BILL PAYMENT

MONTH:					YEAR:	

PAID	BILL DESCRIPTION	DUE DATE	AMOUNT DUE	AMOUNT PAID	UNPAID BALANCE	NOTES
☐						
☐						
☐						
☐						
☐						
☐						
☐						
☐						
☐						
☐						
☐						
☐						
☐						
☐						
☐						
☐						
☐						
☐						
☐						
☐						
☐						
☐						
	TOTAL					

MONTHLY BILL PAYMENT

MONTH:					YEAR:	

PAID	BILL DESCRIPTION	DUE DATE	AMOUNT DUE	AMOUNT PAID	UNPAID BALANCE	NOTES
☐						
☐						
☐						
☐						
☐						
☐						
☐						
☐						
☐						
☐						
☐						
☐						
☐						
☐						
☐						
☐						
☐						
☐						
☐						
☐						
☐						
☐						
☐						
☐						
	TOTAL					

MONTHLY BILL PAYMENT

MONTH:						YEAR:

PAID	BILL DESCRIPTION	DUE DATE	AMOUNT DUE	AMOUNT PAID	UNPAID BALANCE	NOTES
☐						
☐						
☐						
☐						
☐						
☐						
☐						
☐						
☐						
☐						
☐						
☐						
☐						
☐						
☐						
☐						
☐						
☐						
☐						
☐						
☐						
☐						
	TOTAL					

MONTHLY BILL PAYMENT

MONTH:						YEAR:

PAID	BILL DESCRIPTION	DUE DATE	AMOUNT DUE	AMOUNT PAID	UNPAID BALANCE	NOTES
☐						
☐						
☐						
☐						
☐						
☐						
☐						
☐						
☐						
☐						
☐						
☐						
☐						
☐						
☐						
☐						
☐						
☐						
☐						
☐						
☐						
☐						
☐						
☐						
	TOTAL					

MONTHLY BILL PAYMENT

MONTH:						YEAR:

PAID	BILL DESCRIPTION	DUE DATE	AMOUNT DUE	AMOUNT PAID	UNPAID BALANCE	NOTES
☐						
☐						
☐						
☐						
☐						
☐						
☐						
☐						
☐						
☐						
☐						
☐						
☐						
☐						
☐						
☐						
☐						
☐						
☐						
☐						
☐						
☐						
	TOTAL					

MONTHLY BILL PAYMENT

MONTH:					YEAR:	

PAID	BILL DESCRIPTION	DUE DATE	AMOUNT DUE	AMOUNT PAID	UNPAID BALANCE	NOTES
☐						
☐						
☐						
☐						
☐						
☐						
☐						
☐						
☐						
☐						
☐						
☐						
☐						
☐						
☐						
☐						
☐						
☐						
☐						
☐						
☐						
☐						
☐						
	TOTAL					

MONTHLY BILL PAYMENT

MONTH:					YEAR:	

PAID	BILL DESCRIPTION	DUE DATE	AMOUNT DUE	AMOUNT PAID	UNPAID BALANCE	NOTES
☐						
☐						
☐						
☐						
☐						
☐						
☐						
☐						
☐						
☐						
☐						
☐						
☐						
☐						
☐						
☐						
☐						
☐						
☐						
☐						
☐						
☐						
☐						
	TOTAL					

MONTHLY BILL PAYMENT

MONTH:					YEAR:	

PAID	BILL DESCRIPTION	DUE DATE	AMOUNT DUE	AMOUNT PAID	UNPAID BALANCE	NOTES
☐						
☐						
☐						
☐						
☐						
☐						
☐						
☐						
☐						
☐						
☐						
☐						
☐						
☐						
☐						
☐						
☐						
☐						
☐						
☐						
☐						
☐						
☐						
☐						
	TOTAL					

MONTHLY BILL PAYMENT

MONTH:						YEAR:

PAID	BILL DESCRIPTION	DUE DATE	AMOUNT DUE	AMOUNT PAID	UNPAID BALANCE	NOTES
☐						
☐						
☐						
☐						
☐						
☐						
☐						
☐						
☐						
☐						
☐						
☐						
☐						
☐						
☐						
☐						
☐						
☐						
☐						
☐						
☐						
☐						
☐						
	TOTAL					

MONTHLY BILL PAYMENT

MONTH:					YEAR:	

PAID	BILL DESCRIPTION	DUE DATE	AMOUNT DUE	AMOUNT PAID	UNPAID BALANCE	NOTES
☐						
☐						
☐						
☐						
☐						
☐						
☐						
☐						
☐						
☐						
☐						
☐						
☐						
☐						
☐						
☐						
☐						
☐						
☐						
☐						
☐						
☐						
☐						
	TOTAL					

MONTHLY BILL PAYMENT

MONTH:						YEAR:

PAID	BILL DESCRIPTION	DUE DATE	AMOUNT DUE	AMOUNT PAID	UNPAID BALANCE	NOTES
☐						
☐						
☐						
☐						
☐						
☐						
☐						
☐						
☐						
☐						
☐						
☐						
☐						
☐						
☐						
☐						
☐						
☐						
☐						
☐						
☐						
☐						
☐						
	TOTAL					

MONTHLY BILL PAYMENT

MONTH:					YEAR:	

PAID	BILL DESCRIPTION	DUE DATE	AMOUNT DUE	AMOUNT PAID	UNPAID BALANCE	NOTES
☐						
☐						
☐						
☐						
☐						
☐						
☐						
☐						
☐						
☐						
☐						
☐						
☐						
☐						
☐						
☐						
☐						
☐						
☐						
☐						
☐						
☐						
☐						
	TOTAL					

_____

_____

_____

MONTHLY BILL PAYMENT

MONTH:						YEAR:

PAID	BILL DESCRIPTION	DUE DATE	AMOUNT DUE	AMOUNT PAID	UNPAID BALANCE	NOTES
☐						
☐						
☐						
☐						
☐						
☐						
☐						
☐						
☐						
☐						
☐						
☐						
☐						
☐						
☐						
☐						
☐						
☐						
☐						
☐						
☐						
☐						
☐						
	TOTAL					

MONTHLY BILL PAYMENT

MONTH:					YEAR:	

PAID	BILL DESCRIPTION	DUE DATE	AMOUNT DUE	AMOUNT PAID	UNPAID BALANCE	NOTES
☐						
☐						
☐						
☐						
☐						
☐						
☐						
☐						
☐						
☐						
☐						
☐						
☐						
☐						
☐						
☐						
☐						
☐						
☐						
☐						
☐						
☐						
	TOTAL					

MONTHLY BILL PAYMENT

MONTH:						YEAR:

PAID	BILL DESCRIPTION	DUE DATE	AMOUNT DUE	AMOUNT PAID	UNPAID BALANCE	NOTES
☐						
☐						
☐						
☐						
☐						
☐						
☐						
☐						
☐						
☐						
☐						
☐						
☐						
☐						
☐						
☐						
☐						
☐						
☐						
☐						
☐						
☐						
☐						
	TOTAL					

MONTHLY BILL PAYMENT

| MONTH: | | | | | YEAR: | |

PAID	BILL DESCRIPTION	DUE DATE	AMOUNT DUE	AMOUNT PAID	UNPAID BALANCE	NOTES
☐						
☐						
☐						
☐						
☐						
☐						
☐						
☐						
☐						
☐						
☐						
☐						
☐						
☐						
☐						
☐						
☐						
☐						
☐						
☐						
☐						
☐						
☐						
	TOTAL					

MONTHLY BILL PAYMENT

| MONTH: | | | | | | YEAR: |

PAID	BILL DESCRIPTION	DUE DATE	AMOUNT DUE	AMOUNT PAID	UNPAID BALANCE	NOTES
☐						
☐						
☐						
☐						
☐						
☐						
☐						
☐						
☐						
☐						
☐						
☐						
☐						
☐						
☐						
☐						
☐						
☐						
☐						
☐						
☐						
☐						
☐						
	TOTAL					

MONTHLY BILL PAYMENT

MONTH:					YEAR:	

PAID	BILL DESCRIPTION	DUE DATE	AMOUNT DUE	AMOUNT PAID	UNPAID BALANCE	NOTES
☐						
☐						
☐						
☐						
☐						
☐						
☐						
☐						
☐						
☐						
☐						
☐						
☐						
☐						
☐						
☐						
☐						
☐						
☐						
☐						
☐						
☐						
☐						
	TOTAL					

MONTHLY BILL PAYMENT

MONTH:						YEAR:

PAID	BILL DESCRIPTION	DUE DATE	AMOUNT DUE	AMOUNT PAID	UNPAID BALANCE	NOTES
☐						
☐						
☐						
☐						
☐						
☐						
☐						
☐						
☐						
☐						
☐						
☐						
☐						
☐						
☐						
☐						
☐						
☐						
☐						
☐						
☐						
☐						
☐						
	TOTAL					

_____

_____

_____

_____

MONTHLY BILL PAYMENT

MONTH:					YEAR:	

PAID	BILL DESCRIPTION	DUE DATE	AMOUNT DUE	AMOUNT PAID	UNPAID BALANCE	NOTES
☐						
☐						
☐						
☐						
☐						
☐						
☐						
☐						
☐						
☐						
☐						
☐						
☐						
☐						
☐						
☐						
☐						
☐						
☐						
☐						
☐						
☐						
☐						
	TOTAL					

MONTHLY BILL PAYMENT

MONTH:					YEAR:	

PAID	BILL DESCRIPTION	DUE DATE	AMOUNT DUE	AMOUNT PAID	UNPAID BALANCE	NOTES
☐						
☐						
☐						
☐						
☐						
☐						
☐						
☐						
☐						
☐						
☐						
☐						
☐						
☐						
☐						
☐						
☐						
☐						
☐						
☐						
☐						
☐						
☐						
	TOTAL					

MONTHLY BILL PAYMENT

MONTH:					YEAR:	

PAID	BILL DESCRIPTION	DUE DATE	AMOUNT DUE	AMOUNT PAID	UNPAID BALANCE	NOTES
☐						
☐						
☐						
☐						
☐						
☐						
☐						
☐						
☐						
☐						
☐						
☐						
☐						
☐						
☐						
☐						
☐						
☐						
☐						
☐						
☐						
☐						
	TOTAL					

MONTHLY BILL PAYMENT

MONTH:					YEAR:	

PAID	BILL DESCRIPTION	DUE DATE	AMOUNT DUE	AMOUNT PAID	UNPAID BALANCE	NOTES
☐						
☐						
☐						
☐						
☐						
☐						
☐						
☐						
☐						
☐						
☐						
☐						
☐						
☐						
☐						
☐						
☐						
☐						
☐						
☐						
☐						
☐						
☐						
	TOTAL					

MONTHLY BILL PAYMENT

MONTH:					YEAR:	

PAID	BILL DESCRIPTION	DUE DATE	AMOUNT DUE	AMOUNT PAID	UNPAID BALANCE	NOTES
☐						
☐						
☐						
☐						
☐						
☐						
☐						
☐						
☐						
☐						
☐						
☐						
☐						
☐						
☐						
☐						
☐						
☐						
☐						
☐						
☐						
☐						
☐						
	TOTAL					

MONTHLY BILL PAYMENT

MONTH:						YEAR:

PAID	BILL DESCRIPTION	DUE DATE	AMOUNT DUE	AMOUNT PAID	UNPAID BALANCE	NOTES
☐						
☐						
☐						
☐						
☐						
☐						
☐						
☐						
☐						
☐						
☐						
☐						
☐						
☐						
☐						
☐						
☐						
☐						
☐						
☐						
☐						
☐						
☐						
TOTAL						

MONTHLY BILL PAYMENT

MONTH:					YEAR:	

PAID	BILL DESCRIPTION	DUE DATE	AMOUNT DUE	AMOUNT PAID	UNPAID BALANCE	NOTES
☐						
☐						
☐						
☐						
☐						
☐						
☐						
☐						
☐						
☐						
☐						
☐						
☐						
☐						
☐						
☐						
☐						
☐						
☐						
☐						
☐						
☐						
	TOTAL					

MONTHLY BILL PAYMENT

MONTH:					YEAR:	

PAID	BILL DESCRIPTION	DUE DATE	AMOUNT DUE	AMOUNT PAID	UNPAID BALANCE	NOTES
☐						
☐						
☐						
☐						
☐						
☐						
☐						
☐						
☐						
☐						
☐						
☐						
☐						
☐						
☐						
☐						
☐						
☐						
☐						
☐						
☐						
☐						
☐						
	TOTAL					

MONTHLY BILL PAYMENT

MONTH:						YEAR:

PAID	BILL DESCRIPTION	DUE DATE	AMOUNT DUE	AMOUNT PAID	UNPAID BALANCE	NOTES
☐						
☐						
☐						
☐						
☐						
☐						
☐						
☐						
☐						
☐						
☐						
☐						
☐						
☐						
☐						
☐						
☐						
☐						
☐						
☐						
☐						
☐						
☐						
	TOTAL					

MONTHLY BILL PAYMENT

MONTH:						YEAR:

PAID	BILL DESCRIPTION	DUE DATE	AMOUNT DUE	AMOUNT PAID	UNPAID BALANCE	NOTES
☐						
☐						
☐						
☐						
☐						
☐						
☐						
☐						
☐						
☐						
☐						
☐						
☐						
☐						
☐						
☐						
☐						
☐						
☐						
☐						
☐						
☐						
☐						
☐						
	TOTAL					

MONTHLY BILL PAYMENT

MONTH:					YEAR:	

PAID	BILL DESCRIPTION	DUE DATE	AMOUNT DUE	AMOUNT PAID	UNPAID BALANCE	NOTES
☐						
☐						
☐						
☐						
☐						
☐						
☐						
☐						
☐						
☐						
☐						
☐						
☐						
☐						
☐						
☐						
☐						
☐						
☐						
☐						
☐						
☐						
☐						
	TOTAL					

MONTHLY BILL PAYMENT

MONTH:					YEAR:	

PAID	BILL DESCRIPTION	DUE DATE	AMOUNT DUE	AMOUNT PAID	UNPAID BALANCE	NOTES
☐						
☐						
☐						
☐						
☐						
☐						
☐						
☐						
☐						
☐						
☐						
☐						
☐						
☐						
☐						
☐						
☐						
☐						
☐						
☐						
☐						
☐						
☐						
	TOTAL					

MONTHLY BILL PAYMENT

MONTH:					YEAR:	

PAID	BILL DESCRIPTION	DUE DATE	AMOUNT DUE	AMOUNT PAID	UNPAID BALANCE	NOTES
☐						
☐						
☐						
☐						
☐						
☐						
☐						
☐						
☐						
☐						
☐						
☐						
☐						
☐						
☐						
☐						
☐						
☐						
☐						
☐						
☐						
☐						
	TOTAL					

MONTHLY BILL PAYMENT

MONTH:					YEAR:	

PAID	BILL DESCRIPTION	DUE DATE	AMOUNT DUE	AMOUNT PAID	UNPAID BALANCE	NOTES
☐						
☐						
☐						
☐						
☐						
☐						
☐						
☐						
☐						
☐						
☐						
☐						
☐						
☐						
☐						
☐						
☐						
☐						
☐						
☐						
☐						
☐						
☐						
	TOTAL					

MONTHLY BILL PAYMENT

MONTH:					YEAR:	

PAID	BILL DESCRIPTION	DUE DATE	AMOUNT DUE	AMOUNT PAID	UNPAID BALANCE	NOTES
☐						
☐						
☐						
☐						
☐						
☐						
☐						
☐						
☐						
☐						
☐						
☐						
☐						
☐						
☐						
☐						
☐						
☐						
☐						
☐						
☐						
☐						
☐						
TOTAL						

MONTHLY BILL PAYMENT

MONTH:						YEAR:

PAID	BILL DESCRIPTION	DUE DATE	AMOUNT DUE	AMOUNT PAID	UNPAID BALANCE	NOTES
☐						
☐						
☐						
☐						
☐						
☐						
☐						
☐						
☐						
☐						
☐						
☐						
☐						
☐						
☐						
☐						
☐						
☐						
☐						
☐						
☐						
☐						
☐						
	TOTAL					

MONTHLY BILL PAYMENT

MONTH:						YEAR:

PAID	BILL DESCRIPTION	DUE DATE	AMOUNT DUE	AMOUNT PAID	UNPAID BALANCE	NOTES
☐						
☐						
☐						
☐						
☐						
☐						
☐						
☐						
☐						
☐						
☐						
☐						
☐						
☐						
☐						
☐						
☐						
☐						
☐						
☐						
☐						
☐						
☐						
	TOTAL					

MONTHLY BILL PAYMENT

MONTH:						YEAR:

PAID	BILL DESCRIPTION	DUE DATE	AMOUNT DUE	AMOUNT PAID	UNPAID BALANCE	NOTES
☐						
☐						
☐						
☐						
☐						
☐						
☐						
☐						
☐						
☐						
☐						
☐						
☐						
☐						
☐						
☐						
☐						
☐						
☐						
☐						
☐						
☐						
☐						
	TOTAL					

MONTHLY BILL PAYMENT

| MONTH: | | | | | YEAR: | |

PAID	BILL DESCRIPTION	DUE DATE	AMOUNT DUE	AMOUNT PAID	UNPAID BALANCE	NOTES
☐						
☐						
☐						
☐						
☐						
☐						
☐						
☐						
☐						
☐						
☐						
☐						
☐						
☐						
☐						
☐						
☐						
☐						
☐						
☐						
☐						
☐						
☐						
	TOTAL					

MONTHLY BILL PAYMENT

MONTH:						YEAR:

PAID	BILL DESCRIPTION	DUE DATE	AMOUNT DUE	AMOUNT PAID	UNPAID BALANCE	NOTES
☐						
☐						
☐						
☐						
☐						
☐						
☐						
☐						
☐						
☐						
☐						
☐						
☐						
☐						
☐						
☐						
☐						
☐						
☐						
☐						
☐						
☐						
	TOTAL					

MONTHLY BILL PAYMENT

MONTH:					YEAR:	

PAID	BILL DESCRIPTION	DUE DATE	AMOUNT DUE	AMOUNT PAID	UNPAID BALANCE	NOTES
☐						
☐						
☐						
☐						
☐						
☐						
☐						
☐						
☐						
☐						
☐						
☐						
☐						
☐						
☐						
☐						
☐						
☐						
☐						
☐						
☐						
☐						
☐						
☐						
TOTAL						

MONTHLY BILL PAYMENT

MONTH:						YEAR:

PAID	BILL DESCRIPTION	DUE DATE	AMOUNT DUE	AMOUNT PAID	UNPAID BALANCE	NOTES
☐						
☐						
☐						
☐						
☐						
☐						
☐						
☐						
☐						
☐						
☐						
☐						
☐						
☐						
☐						
☐						
☐						
☐						
☐						
☐						
☐						
☐						
☐						
	TOTAL					

MONTHLY BILL PAYMENT

MONTH:						YEAR:

PAID	BILL DESCRIPTION	DUE DATE	AMOUNT DUE	AMOUNT PAID	UNPAID BALANCE	NOTES
☐						
☐						
☐						
☐						
☐						
☐						
☐						
☐						
☐						
☐						
☐						
☐						
☐						
☐						
☐						
☐						
☐						
☐						
☐						
☐						
☐						
☐						
☐						
	TOTAL					

MONTHLY BILL PAYMENT

MONTH:					YEAR:	

PAID	BILL DESCRIPTION	DUE DATE	AMOUNT DUE	AMOUNT PAID	UNPAID BALANCE	NOTES
☐						
☐						
☐						
☐						
☐						
☐						
☐						
☐						
☐						
☐						
☐						
☐						
☐						
☐						
☐						
☐						
☐						
☐						
☐						
☐						
☐						
☐						
	TOTAL					

MONTHLY BILL PAYMENT

MONTH:					YEAR:	

PAID	BILL DESCRIPTION	DUE DATE	AMOUNT DUE	AMOUNT PAID	UNPAID BALANCE	NOTES
☐						
☐						
☐						
☐						
☐						
☐						
☐						
☐						
☐						
☐						
☐						
☐						
☐						
☐						
☐						
☐						
☐						
☐						
☐						
☐						
☐						
☐						
☐						
	TOTAL					

MONTHLY BILL PAYMENT

MONTH:						YEAR:

PAID	BILL DESCRIPTION	DUE DATE	AMOUNT DUE	AMOUNT PAID	UNPAID BALANCE	NOTES
☐						
☐						
☐						
☐						
☐						
☐						
☐						
☐						
☐						
☐						
☐						
☐						
☐						
☐						
☐						
☐						
☐						
☐						
☐						
☐						
☐						
☐						
☐						
☐						
	TOTAL					

MONTHLY BILL PAYMENT

MONTH:					YEAR:	

PAID	BILL DESCRIPTION	DUE DATE	AMOUNT DUE	AMOUNT PAID	UNPAID BALANCE	NOTES
☐						
☐						
☐						
☐						
☐						
☐						
☐						
☐						
☐						
☐						
☐						
☐						
☐						
☐						
☐						
☐						
☐						
☐						
☐						
☐						
☐						
☐						
☐						
	TOTAL					

MONTHLY BILL PAYMENT

MONTH:						YEAR:

PAID	BILL DESCRIPTION	DUE DATE	AMOUNT DUE	AMOUNT PAID	UNPAID BALANCE	NOTES
☐						
☐						
☐						
☐						
☐						
☐						
☐						
☐						
☐						
☐						
☐						
☐						
☐						
☐						
☐						
☐						
☐						
☐						
☐						
☐						
☐						
☐						
☐						
	TOTAL					

MONTHLY BILL PAYMENT

MONTH:					YEAR:	

PAID	BILL DESCRIPTION	DUE DATE	AMOUNT DUE	AMOUNT PAID	UNPAID BALANCE	NOTES
☐						
☐						
☐						
☐						
☐						
☐						
☐						
☐						
☐						
☐						
☐						
☐						
☐						
☐						
☐						
☐						
☐						
☐						
☐						
☐						
☐						
☐						
☐						
	TOTAL					

MONTHLY BILL PAYMENT

| MONTH: | | | | | YEAR: | |

PAID	BILL DESCRIPTION	DUE DATE	AMOUNT DUE	AMOUNT PAID	UNPAID BALANCE	NOTES
☐						
☐						
☐						
☐						
☐						
☐						
☐						
☐						
☐						
☐						
☐						
☐						
☐						
☐						
☐						
☐						
☐						
☐						
☐						
☐						
☐						
☐						
☐						
☐						
TOTAL						

MONTHLY BILL PAYMENT

MONTH:						YEAR:

PAID	BILL DESCRIPTION	DUE DATE	AMOUNT DUE	AMOUNT PAID	UNPAID BALANCE	NOTES
☐						
☐						
☐						
☐						
☐						
☐						
☐						
☐						
☐						
☐						
☐						
☐						
☐						
☐						
☐						
☐						
☐						
☐						
☐						
☐						
☐						
☐						
	TOTAL					

MONTHLY BILL PAYMENT

MONTH:						YEAR:

PAID	BILL DESCRIPTION	DUE DATE	AMOUNT DUE	AMOUNT PAID	UNPAID BALANCE	NOTES
☐						
☐						
☐						
☐						
☐						
☐						
☐						
☐						
☐						
☐						
☐						
☐						
☐						
☐						
☐						
☐						
☐						
☐						
☐						
☐						
☐						
☐						
☐						
	TOTAL					

MONTHLY BILL PAYMENT

MONTH:						YEAR:

PAID	BILL DESCRIPTION	DUE DATE	AMOUNT DUE	AMOUNT PAID	UNPAID BALANCE	NOTES
☐						
☐						
☐						
☐						
☐						
☐						
☐						
☐						
☐						
☐						
☐						
☐						
☐						
☐						
☐						
☐						
☐						
☐						
☐						
☐						
☐						
☐						
☐						
	TOTAL					

MONTHLY BILL PAYMENT

MONTH:						YEAR:

PAID	BILL DESCRIPTION	DUE DATE	AMOUNT DUE	AMOUNT PAID	UNPAID BALANCE	NOTES
☐						
☐						
☐						
☐						
☐						
☐						
☐						
☐						
☐						
☐						
☐						
☐						
☐						
☐						
☐						
☐						
☐						
☐						
☐						
☐						
☐						
☐						
☐						
☐						
	TOTAL					

MONTHLY BILL PAYMENT

MONTH:						YEAR:

PAID	BILL DESCRIPTION	DUE DATE	AMOUNT DUE	AMOUNT PAID	UNPAID BALANCE	NOTES
☐						
☐						
☐						
☐						
☐						
☐						
☐						
☐						
☐						
☐						
☐						
☐						
☐						
☐						
☐						
☐						
☐						
☐						
☐						
☐						
☐						
☐						
☐						
	TOTAL					

MONTHLY BILL PAYMENT

MONTH:					YEAR:	

PAID	BILL DESCRIPTION	DUE DATE	AMOUNT DUE	AMOUNT PAID	UNPAID BALANCE	NOTES
☐						
☐						
☐						
☐						
☐						
☐						
☐						
☐						
☐						
☐						
☐						
☐						
☐						
☐						
☐						
☐						
☐						
☐						
☐						
☐						
☐						
☐						
	TOTAL					

MONTHLY BILL PAYMENT

MONTH:						YEAR:

PAID	BILL DESCRIPTION	DUE DATE	AMOUNT DUE	AMOUNT PAID	UNPAID BALANCE	NOTES
☐						
☐						
☐						
☐						
☐						
☐						
☐						
☐						
☐						
☐						
☐						
☐						
☐						
☐						
☐						
☐						
☐						
☐						
☐						
☐						
☐						
☐						
☐						
	TOTAL					

www.ingramcontent.com/pod-product-compliance
Lightning Source LLC
Chambersburg PA
CBHW051758200326
41597CB00025B/4605